Contents

Introduction 1
False dilemmas and poisoned wells.. 3
Selective evidence and complex questions... 5
From the particular to the general, moderate views and affirmations 9
Weasel words, false causes and slippery slopes 12
Getting an *ought* from an *is* and conditional arguments..................................... 16
Another conditional argument and appeals to force 19
Begging the question and straw man 21
Red herrings and attacking the person.. 24
Majority belief and perfectionists... 27
Weak analogies and appeals to ignorance 29

Introduction

The media frequently report on rogue salespeople. The problem of dishonest salespeople persists across a wide range of industries. There are of course many sales organisations operating honestly and ethically. However, just because an organisation believes it teaches ethical practice it does not mean they do. In fact, many salespeople believe they are selling honestly when in truth they are not. This book exposes the top ten sales tricks used intentionally by dishonest salespeople, but also unintentionally by some 'honest' salespeople. But why do those who believe they are honest and ethical often sell dishonestly?

The reason is because some salespeople rely on a sales presentation, or more accurately a methodology, which is geared toward the art of rhetoric. Now, rhetoric has a particular emphasis on persuasion and motivation rather than on establishing genuine needs and imparting truthful and accurate information. As a consequence salespeople learn to use all the tricks of rhetorical arguments. The problem is not a new one. Plato criticised the Sophists for using rhetoric as a means of deceit instead of discovering the truth. Having been a salesman and taught selling skills for over twenty years I can confirm Plato would say the same today of modern sales practices.

So, claiming to sell ethically and selling ethically are not the same. Moreover, salesmanship is often thought of as being about the rules of rhetoric rather than discovering the facts and genuine needs of the buyer.

It should be said that salespeople are not alone in attracting criticism for their reliance on rhetoric. Rhetoric is used in all spheres of life; politics and advertising are two obvious examples, so also in the social science. Even in those areas where we expect to find objective testing and reporting of facts we find people are not immune from the problems inherent in the art of rhetoric. For example, when scientists attempt to persuade their peers to accept their findings they do so with reasoned arguments. These arguments are intended to show how their study or experiment resulted in sufficient evidence to support their conclusions. But their arguments are not always flawless; quite the contrary. They can also be informed by bias, prejudice, or just plain spurious lines of reasoning.

Problems arise in the sales environment because salespeople attempt, seemingly, to present us with a reasoned argument to buy a product or service. Arguments are of course essential to finding out which view is better so we can then make a rational choice. However, what graces the pages of many sales textbooks as exemplars of effective selling techniques are in fact simply a catalogue of the 'bad' rules of argument. This brings us to the heart of the problem. Because of the persuasive nature of these 'bad' arguments consumers are not given the opportunity to make an informed choice. Instead we are, unintentionally, in many cases, manipulated into a decision.

Assessing the worth of any proposal presented by a salesperson requires examination of the supporting reasons offered. So a good argument allows us to ask whether the evidence offered is relevant to the proposition; and whether the evidence itself is sound. Propositions, reasons and evidence are the constituent parts of any sound argument. Without these we are merely being offered a piece of propaganda, prejudice, or something worse, masquerading as an argument. But we cannot decide between competing conclusions by consulting our respective prejudices. These cannot be assessed or inspected in the same way evidence can.

What we want from a salesperson is sound advice presented in the form of a sound argument – *a set of reasons or evidence in support of a conclusion*. Only this gives us as consumers the opportunity to make an informed decision.

Ideally, then, arguments for and against a particular conclusion should be assessed to determine how strong they are. If the salesperson is unable to provide stronger reasons in support of his conclusion than those we offer against it then we should not buy.

However, this is seldom what actually happens. Sales presentations are often not rational processes, but rather emotive ones. While we might reasonably expect advice following logically from the reasons or premises to a conclusion, what we get is often anything but logical. Under these circumstances there are often no good reasons to buy, yet we do. The reason we buy when we shouldn't is because it is often too much effort on our part to weigh the evidence. In fact the salesperson is counting on our laziness. But even if we are willing we often fail to spot the flaws in the salesperson's argument. As a result we are persuaded to buy by mere plausibility.

So, this guide to the Top 10 Sales Tricks will help you spot the most common bad arguments used to persuade us to buy when we shouldn't. To this end I will examine two types of unethical selling frequently committed by salespeople - *fallacies* and *rhetorical ploys*. A fallacy is simply a violation of one of the rules of good argument, or is a mistake in the line reasoning. A rhetorical ploy is non-argumentative reasoning that masquerades as justification for accepting a claim.

By exposing these 'tricks of the trade' I will show just how unsound some arguments used by honest and dishonest salespeople alike can be. If they are unsound we should not be persuaded.

Let us first look at some classic examples of rhetorical arguments designed to manipulate rather than provide justification for buying a product or service.

CHAPTER 1

False dilemmas and poisoned wells

In the introduction I said a sales presentation is essentially an argument; often an unreasoned argument that fails to provide a convincing case to buy. Instead rhetorical ploys are used to manipulate the conclusion. This invariably is that you need to buy the product or service on offer.

In this chapter I will look at two very common 'tricks' or logical fallacies to illustrate how a salesperson can make the case for buying their product or service more compelling than it actually is.

The false dilemma:

In formal terms the argument looks like this: either A or B, not B, therefore A. Now there is nothing intrinsically wrong with the structure of such arguments, so long as the alternatives on offer to us are the only alternatives. Here's a classic example.

> Either we cut welfare or the government goes into the red. We cannot allow the government to go into the red. Therefore, we must cut welfare.

Here we are forced, perhaps unreasonably, to accept the conclusion when there are other alternatives the Government can explore; e.g. increase taxes, cut defence spending and so on. However, the way the argument is presented to us has already concluded that welfare should be cut. But the case has clearly not been made honestly if it relies on a false premise; namely the assumption these are the Governments' only alternatives.

Either/or type arguments are common in sales presentations particularly when closing the sale. Again, there is nothing fundamentally wrong with the structure, just the content.

> Either you take out payment protection insurance (PPI) on your loan, or you risk losing your home if you are ill. You don't want to lose your home, do you? So, you need PPI.

Or take this example I heard recently involving a claim that the National Grid will cease to function in the near future.

> Either you buy this solar panel heating system, or you will be without any form of power in the future. You don't want to be without heating and lighting do you? Therefore, you must install the system.

These arguments have been simplified for illustrative purposes. But in each case we have a closing argument that attempts to foster the idea there are just two alternatives when clearly there are others. It is not surprising given the prevalence of such arguments in sales presentations that the *false dilemma* is often referred to in textbooks as *the salesperson's trick.*

Any salesperson knowingly creating a false dilemma is fundamentally dishonest. But even offered unwittingly they are still grossly misleading and manipulative. The alternatives offered are not a true indication of our actual choices. Instead it is an attempt to railroad us into making a choice between false alternatives with only one possible outcome – we must buy.

As consumers we need to be aware of what choices we are being offered. In particular we need to be on guard against arguments offering us an either/or choice. They are unlikely be the only choices.

Poisoning the well:

Another common practice is the use of loaded language. This is used to disparage any dissenting argument we might have for not buying; often before we even mention it. In the sales books this is known as *anticipating the objection.* By using this kind of argument the salesperson attempts to make his argument look good and any opposing position implausible, false, or absurd. Hence, *poisoning the well*.

If we are uncertain about whether to a purchase a service contract on an expensive item we are not necessarily 'leaving our future prosperity to chance'. Similarly, we may be hesitant about whether or not to purchase private health care, but this does not necessarily mean we are 'taking a risk with our family's future'.

What we require from salespeople is an honest argument where the reasons and evidence in favour of their proposals can be assessed and verified. Arguments whose only function is to sway the emotions of the consumer are manipulative. Such arguments might be effective but hardly fair. But here's an interesting point often overlooked in the quest for sales. Fair and honest arguments also have the power to persuade!

So be vigilant when the salesman comes to call – *caveat emptor* - *false dilemmas* and *poisoned wells*.

CHAPTER 2

Selective evidence and complex questions

Sales presentations often contain rhetorical ploys. If spotted they can expose the weakness of the case being presented.

Selective evidence:

When sources of evidences are used to support claims made in a sales presentation that evidence needs to be appropriate, not selective. When it is selective we are being coerced into committing ourselves to an underlying claim that is not wholly supported by the facts.

Proof by *selective evidence* is an extremely common form of dishonest argument. In selecting evidence to support the worth or claims being made the salesperson presents to us only those pieces of evidence that shine a favourable light on their product or service. To add credibility to the worth of the claims made salespeople will often select independent sources. Such evidence might be a report in a newspaper or a trade journal. It might refer to an opinion poll. This has all the hallmarks of openness or transparency. But where are the independent reports that are not so favourable? Who commissioned the opinion poll?

However, I am sure if we sought out a competitor they too will have newspaper and trade journal reports which say how wonderful their product or service is. They might also have an opinion poll showing how they are preferred by eight out of ten users. Both companies can't be the best. So where does the truth lay?

We should seek out counter-claims whenever possible. Do some online research, ask users of the product or service what their experiences have been. When selective evidence is deployed, the end being served by the salesperson is not the facts, but their own substantive interests.

Offering proof by selected instances is an attempt to present incomplete for complete evidence upon which we are supposed to make a decision; invariably favourable to the salesperson. Selected instances of this sort have no place in a sales presentation.

There are of course times when we know we must decide on certain purchases. Yet this no reason to settle for selective, and so incomplete, evidence. We should not be persuaded by selective instances that are favourable to the seller's own ends, while ignoring the possibility of other instances that may not be so favourable. Claims need to be backed up and be subjected to testing when possible. We should do what you can to substantiate those claims being made rather than rely on the salesperson to merely stipulate them. We can help our own cause by doing some research in advance. If a salesperson is calling at your home ask around. Ask those you know if they have an experience of the company. Go online and do some research. Ask if you can speak to an existing customer to corroborate their claims. Be prepared to challenge the claims being made for the product or service.

There are of course instances when complete evidence does not exist. No one can know for certain what the stock markets will do in the future. No one can say for sure how interest rates will vary. No one can be sure what the state of the economy will be in twenty or thirty years. What our health will be next week. However, on practical questions of importance we should attempt to gather as much evidence for and against a decision as we can, and then make a decision.

Complex questions:

This is an extremely common ploy among salespeople. It works like this: the salesperson poses a question in such a way that we can neither agree nor disagree without committing to the claim being made.

Complex questions, or the *many questions fallacy*, although often manipulative, sometimes unethical, and improper do nevertheless have legitimate uses. They are often used in the form of leading questions by lawyers, police officers and journalist. They are essentially leading questions which are assumptive, implicative or intimidating.

However embedded in sales presentations assumptive questions are designed to take for granted the very question under discussion. The strategy being it is easier to start with a question that assumes the point you are seeking to make. This then makes it very difficult for the customer to think outside the scope of the question.

A classic example used to illustrate this is:

> Are you still beating your spouse?'

Now, whatever way we answer we commit ourselves to the underlying claim - we are, or were, beating our spouse.

What we need to be aware of is any questions asked that presupposes something that has not been proven or accepted. For example:

> Would you prefer the delivery on Tuesday or Wednesday?
>
> Would you like it in red or green?
>
> Do you want two or three copies?
>
> Will you be investing three or four thousand?
>
> Will you be paying by cash or debit card?

In these examples the complex question closes down debate as to whether we are going to buy. It assumes it is a done deal.

Embedded in a sales presentation the complex question shuts down other possibilities and confines an issue within narrow limits toward a predetermined end. But they are no more than tricks committing us to something we may not, given a fair question, agree to.

So obvious are these traps it is a wonder we fall for them, but we do. The reason they work is because they are asserted in confident and suggestive tones so as to imply they are the only choices - they are not. The only way of meeting the difficulty is to call into question the fallacious assumption being made.

Appeals to authority:

There are times when it would be right to heed the advice of an authority, others times not. If a pharmacist warns us not to drive when taking a prescribed drug, we would be foolhardy, and irresponsible to ignore that advice. But often appeals to authority are fallacious. If the same pharmacist advised me to invest in pork bellies I might want to get a second opinion, or at the very least establish their credentials in pork belly futures market.

During a sales presentation there are times when corroborative evidence might be useful to support a claim. The use of such evidence often comes in the form of an appeal to authority. Yet often what or who is being presented as an authority lacks the appropriate expertise or impartiality so we should not be too easily persuaded.

When celebrity endorsements are used as appeals to authority we need to be wary. Why should a celebrity know more about the effectiveness of a given product than you or I? Where they paid? Despite the highly questionable credentials of some 'authorities' we still find them being ranged against us in the drive for new business.

Another appeal to authority might be a list of blue chip clients using a particular product or service. But why should a company that makes aeroplanes, or bicycles be any more of an expert in photocopying supplies, heating equipment, or health plans than anyone else? Even in those cases when it might be argued that the client in question is an authority it is highly unlikely they use the services of just one company. And what about the other blue chip companies not on the list? Who are they buying from? Presumably these other companies thought a competitor offered a better product or service.

Whenever corroborative evidence is used it seems reasonable we should be able to satisfy ourselves on a number of issues. Is the source informed? Is the source impartial? Can the source be cross-checked? Not everyone will want to do this, and this is why the salesperson often gets away with questionable authority sources as supporting evidence.

However, not all appeals to authority are quite so overt. For example statements which take the form:

> Everybody knows that ...

> All my clients prefer to …

> Anyone who does … also does …

These are also appeals to authority. When such statements are used they are supposed to persuade us without giving a reason to show that 'everybody', 'all' and 'anyone' are an informed or impartial source.

To avoid being swayed by such statements we need to ask ourselves whether there is any good reason for supposing that in this case 'everybody', 'all', or 'anyone' is right. Simply being in the majority doesn't make you right.

Another variation of the appeal to authority is to say something like:

> This is how it has always been done.

> We have always done it this way.

Perhaps so, but it is not unreasonable for us to ask ourselves whether in light of new knowledge, or a new product, we have a reason to revise the way we have done things in the past.

We can, and should, do all we can to ensure decisions made are sound and free from appeals to questionable authorities.

Informed decision-making requires we have all the information necessary to make that decision. Being offered selective evidence, or asked trick questions, or being offered dubious authority sources are invariably attempts to get us to make a favourable, but ill-informed, decision.

CHAPTER 3

From the particular to the general, moderate views and affirmations

In our continued look at the often unfair and foul nature of some sales presentations three more common fallacies or mistakes in reasoning will be examined. Spurious reasoning may be an honest mistake by a salesperson, we were not all trained in the subtle art of Rhetoric. But it is convenient if it makes more plausible what a more substantive argument might not. Questionable reasoning then becomes a device which denies us the right to make informed decisions about what is the right course of action to take.

From the particular to the general:

This is a weak piece of inductive reasoning which moves from the particular to the general. For example a salesperson attempts to undermine a product or company by a single instance, e.g.; 'a friend of mine had a terrible experience with ....' But there is not a single company in the world that has not had some complaint lodged against it. But this is not a compelling argument that the company offers a bad service or product.

Despite the obvious shortcomings of such arguments some salespeople still use it to try and persuade us to buy their product or service. It typically occurs when they cite examples drawn from personal or professional experience. There is nothing essentially wrong with drawing on first-hand experience. But when offered as a substitute for a substantive argument we should not be persuaded. For example:

> I know a woman who was declined a loan by XYZ bank and her business went bust.

What does this prove? It may actually be proof XYZ bank is a good judge of a viable business rather than a malicious cause of the poor woman losing her business.

> I know someone whose house was robbed three times after they decided not to install shootbolts multipoint locking on their windows.

This claim may be true but on its own does not provide a sufficient enough reason to suppose the house would not have been burgled anyway. Before we can make a fair assessment of any product or service we need background information, anecdotal or apocryphal evidence alone isn't enough.

The moderate view:

An argument recommending an intermediate position between two extremes is not a bad position to take for any salesperson. It makes them seem reasonable, fair-minded, and honest. Indeed, the idea of a compromise has a certain appeal. We might even view the salesperson as being reasonable and sensible. Yet whenever the intermediate position forms the basis of an argument we need to be wary of the *moderate view fallacy*. Organisations offering the most diverse products and opinions can all claim to take the moderate position.

Suppose, for example, we are looking to invest a capital sum: deposit-based organisations represent themselves as the mean between cash and unit trusts; unit trust companies the mean between deposits and equities; equities the mean between unit trusts and futures markets, and so on.

But as *means* they all are right and none of them are right. In other words, they are all the right decision for someone and all the wrong decision for someone else. There is nothing in each being posited as a mean that makes them the right course of action

Take as another example. Suppose one double glazing firm recommends changing all the doors and windows in the house. Another suggests changing just the doors. A third suggests a mid-point between the two. Now this moderate view might seem reasonable. If it means we begin the process of effectively insulating and securing our home when we otherwise wouldn't. So perhaps there is something to commend the moderate view.

However, the problem resides in the idea that truth, or in this case what is the right course of action for us, lies always in the mean position between two extremes. Yet no matter how convenient this may be for the fortunate salesperson, it is of no practical use as a criterion for discovering the right course of action for us. This is because every piece of advice or course of action can be expressed as the mean between too extremes. For example, we are trapped in the desert. We know there is a town to the North and a town to the West and so certain or survival if we reach one or the other. But we cannot decide which way to go. A salesperson suggests we head North West, the mean between the two. What would you do?

What is the best advice is just as likely to lie at one extreme as in the middle position. The *moderate view fallacy* is a common one and often expressed as being the voice of reason. We should of course not suppose that every mean between two extremes is a dishonest argument.

But this moderate view becomes a dishonest argument when it is suggested that the advice *ought* to be taken because it *is* the mean between two extremes. The right advice can always be expressed as a mean between two extremes, but it is not the right advice *because* it is a mean.

The right advice ought to flow from a careful analysis of our particular needs, and what makes it acceptable are the reasons and evidence offered in support. There is nothing essentially wrong with advice that is contrasted, but don't suppose the advice given is the *right* advice simply because it *is* the mean between extremes.

Repeated affirmation:

The repeated affirmation fallacy occurs when a salesperson simply says the thing to be believed over and over again. Now the very idea we might be persuaded by such blatant repetition of a single phrase or statement is preposterous. Granted, few salespeople would be foolhardy enough to simply repeat the same statement in an attempt to persuade us. However, this does not mean that many sales presentations do not rely on repeated affirmations as a substitute for a substantive argument.

Take for example the salesperson who wants to convey the idea of financial security. Throughout the sales presentation they may say something like:

> Only good loft insulation will reduce future energy bills.
>
> Without proper loft insulation your future finances may become uncertain.
>
> Securing your finances with this product will give you peace of mind.

Though differently worded these statements contain nothing but the single idea with which the salesperson started. Yet there is nothing in repeated affirmation to indicate we have any additional reason to buy. While it might be insisted that each of these statements is true they rely for their persuasive force on the idea of repetition and suggestibility, not argument.

Loft insulation and reduce energy bills may well be what we need but our being convinced of the need should not rely on suggestibility but the facts supported by evidence. This of course is just what the use of repeated affirmations is designed to avoid. Providing supporting evidence is a laborious approach for those salespeople preferring quick results; and it works. Some of us prefer to act blindly under the weight of repetition. But if we want to make informed decisions we need to be aware of repeated affirmations, and the usual clue is the absence of an argument.

It does not seem unreasonable to demand from a salesperson advice supported by sound reasoning. Yet, well intentioned as some salespeople may be, they may themselves be completely unaware they are committing these errors in reasoning, or resorting to tried and tested rhetorical ploys to persuade us. If they are unaware of what they are doing then we need to be doubly aware.

CHAPTER 4

Weasel words, false causes and slippery slopes

While it would be desirable if salespeople presented us with reasoned arguments upon which we could base our decisions, it is not something we can rely upon. We must take what comes. However, this does not mean we have to accept what comes if it is questionable definitions, or implausible explanations about what the future holds.

Weasel words:

Keeping to the point is excellent advice for any salesperson to adhere too. But sometimes they find it difficult to do so. If arguments are ill-thought out there is a tendency to change the meaning of a word in the middle of the argument so that the conclusion can be maintained. These *vague* or *weasel words* usually appear in an argument when we put the salesperson under the pressure of a counterexample. For example:

> Salesperson: All investments carry some risk.
> Customer: What about deposit based funds?
> Salesperson: Well that's not really an investment.

Here 'investment' is the weasel word. The salesperson's response to the customer's counterexample in effect changes the meaning of 'investment' to 'investment that exposes the capital sum to risk'. The first statement remains true, but only at the cost of becoming trivially true. It is tantamount to saying 'all investment which are risky are risky' – a meaningless statement.

Take the following example:

> Salesperson: All businesses are interested in making a profit.
> Customer: What about non-profit organisations.
> Salesperson: Well they are not really businesses.

Here 'business' is the weasel word. The salesperson's response to the counterexample has changed the meaning of 'businesses' to 'businesses which make a profit'. Again this is only trivially true and amounts only to saying 'every business which makes a profit makes a profit' – another meaningless statement.

Making a key term vague - either broadening or narrowing its definition to maintain a conclusion undermines the credibility of an argument and we should be suitably unimpressed. We might not be able to prevent salespeople using weasel words but we can insist they be clear about any terms they use, and then insist they only use them as defined. If not we should refuse to accept the meaningless claims they then make to justify the advice given.

Whether the use of weasel words is a consequence of shoddy thinking, or a deliberate attempt to deceive, they have no place in an honest sales presentation. More to the point, whether we are deceived unintentionally or intentionally the use of weasel words still misrepresents the truth.

False causes:

It is not uncommon for salespeople to explain why something happened by arguing about causes. However, what causes what is not always as clear cut as we are often led to believe. It is hard enough in everyday life to know just what caused what to occur. But when used in the narrow confines of a sales presentation we need to be especially on our guard as we might find we are parted with our money by an argument based on a convenient fiction.

If we are asked to make important decisions based on a false understanding of what causes what we are either being ill-advised or misled. While the former may be the result of ignorance, the latter is clearly dishonest.

The following argument seems plausible:

> The number of people claiming on their long-term illness policy is rising each year. With more people than ever being prone to long-term illness it is important you take out long-term sickness protection.

In support of the claim of rising claims the salesperson might even produce statistical evidence as proof. The evidence might even be from a very wide variety of sources and respected authorities. But are the increased claims a result of the general deterioration of public health? Most events have a number of possible causes. But a plausible cause for the increased claims rate is not enough. The increased number of claims might just as easily be explained by an increased number of policyholders. Therefore the reason there are more claims is because there are more policyholders, not more people are prone to long-term illness. In fact the incidence of long-term illness among the population might actually be falling but the claims rate still rising.

The salesperson must go on to show that increased long-term illness among the population is the cause of increased claims. Only then can we access the risk and decide if we ought to take appropriate action. Without appropriate evidence to support this particular claim we have nothing firm upon which to basis our decision. Fairy tales are not the stuff upon which informed decisions should be made.

Some causal arguments offered by salespeople are just coincidental rather than necessarily related. For example:

> Since launching our new 'mortgage plus' product sales have soared. The public response to this new product shows we have listened to our customers and responded with a first rate product.

Once again the salesperson might support the claim by providing evidence of the increased number of sales since the product launched. But is the soundness of the product the most likely cause of increased sales? Could it just be coincidental? Perhaps the product was launched during a peak period in the mortgage cycle - quite possible if the marketing department had anything to do with it.

Additional evidence is often necessary before any explanation of a direct causal link can be accepted with any degree of confidence. Causal explanations are often very persuasive, but not always true. We need to ask whether there might be another explanation for the claim being made. If there is then the initial explanation loses its persuasive force.

The slippery slope:

A slippery slope argument gets going when we are led by the salesperson to acknowledge that a difference between two things is not really significant. The slippery slope argument is a particularly inviting trap when the first step is the easiest to make. For example:

> If tomorrow morning you woke up and found you had 25 pence less in your pocket than you thought, would that alter the quality of your life? What if it was only 50 pence, would that alter your quality of life? Would a pound make a difference? Of course not, so £30 a month is easily affordable!

The basic idea with this type of argument is to get us to make a series of small concessions acknowledging that it is a difference that makes no difference. However, as an argument it does not follow from the fact that a pound is an insignificant sum that £360 a year is insignificant. More to the point, whether we can afford to spend £30 a month is not a reason on its own to buy the product; something more is needed.

Another version of the slippery slope argument is the domino effect. This type of argument is often based on the premise that there is a causal link between sequences of events until a 'horrible' outcome befalls us. This is not to deny that a causal link exists between events, clearly everything that happens has some cause. But what makes this a fallacy, or dishonest trick, is when we are led to take what *might* occur at each stage to the conclusion that the last 'horrible' step *will* happen - unless of course we take immediate action to prevent it. For example:

> I can understand your reluctance to make a hasty decision. But suppose you sit on this for a day or two, then suppose you feel unwell and your doctor recommends a medical check-up, perhaps even an ECG. Then you decide to go ahead with the life policy. The delay might be costly. Because of your recent visit to the doctor we will probably insist on a medical examination. Our underwriters might load the premium. The cost might then be too high so you can't afford the policy. Should you die uninsured this *will* have a negative impact on your children's education and future prospects. Is that what you want?

No salesperson should offer an argument that infers from what *might* happen to what *will* happen. Such arguments are rightly termed fallacious, erroneous and implausible and so there is no reason why we should be persuaded when they are used.

When a salesperson starts to string together a causal chain of events be aware of the subtle change in such arguments moving from a sequence of *mights* to a *will*. If not you might end up with a fantasy story.

We might not have a choice about how salespeople present their arguments to us. But we can examine closely the structure and content of the arguments deployed against us. Just because an argument sounds plausible it doesn't necessarily mean it is plausible let alone true. When words change their meaning, fictions act as convenient causes and slopes become increasingly slippery all add up to fairy tale sales presentations.

CHAPTER 5

Getting an *ought* from an *is* and conditional arguments

During a sales presentation errors in reasoning are not always easy to spot. However, they do undermine their persuasive force and should make us question the salesperson's motives. The salesperson may not knowingly be offering us spurious arguments but just simply applying a sales methodology that is almost standard across all fields of selling. Standard it might be, but non-manipulative it is not. But even if questionable practices are used unknowingly they are not entirely forgivable. They remain manipulative whether used knowingly or unknowingly, just as a brick landing on our head will hurt just as much if accidentally rather than purposefully dropped. It is incumbent upon us as consumers to wear our hard consumer hat and assess the arguments presented.

Deriving ought from is:

A common mistake salespeople make is to blur the fact-value distinction. There is a fundamental difference between how something *is* and how it *ought* to be. The fact that some people save for retirement is one thing; that they should, or *ought* to, is quite another matter. The first just happens to be a fact, the other a matter of value.

Problems occur when salespeople infer an *ought* from an *is*. The following argument seems reasonable:

> How can anyone claim travel insurance is a bad idea? Travel insurance has been around for hundreds of years.

Reasonable as it sounds, it is a fallacious argument. If we look closely at the argument we will see that it makes the following claim:

Travel insurance has existed for hundreds of years. (is)
So it is a good idea (for you). (ought)

This argument has derived an *ought* from an *is* in that it offers a prescriptive conclusion. In other words, it offers as a conclusion what we *ought* to believe solely on the basis that travel insurance has been around for hundreds of years. That there is something wrong, or inadequate, with the argument becomes more apparent if we substitute the following identical argument:

> How can anyone think poverty is a bad thing? Poverty has existed for thousands of years.

Poverty may have existed for centuries, but surely false to suggest it *ought* to be regarded as a good thing. If we are not prepared to accept this conclusion we have exactly the same reason to reject the first argument. Just because something *is* the case does not provide sufficient grounds for concluding something *ought* to be the case.

The reason travel insurance is a good thing, if it is a good thing for you, is because it provides you with protection of a particular kind not covered by any other form of insurance. Not because it has been around for hundreds of years. But if holiday insurance simply covers what might already be covered on your household policy, or a policy offered with a bank account, then the policy on offer is a waste of money, so you *ought* not to buy it.

What we have in both examples is an inference from a descriptive premise (what *is* the case) to a prescriptive conclusion (what *ought* to be the case). Sales presentations that argue that because something *is* the case often do not provide sufficient grounds for why we *ought* to take action. They simply blur the waters to lead us to the conclusion they prescribe.

Conditional arguments:

There is nothing wrong with arguments presented to us which are conditional in that the reasons offered support the conclusion. Conditional arguments are often quite easy to spot. The salesperson will often use the phrase 'If ... then ...' For example:

> If you have poor insulation, then your heating bills will be high.
> Your heating bills are high.
> Therefore, you have poor insulation.

The fairly straight-forward example used to explain the problem with some conditional arguments is the following:

> If it is raining, the windows will be wet
> The windows are wet
> Therefore, it's raining.

However, not all such arguments are as they first appear and you might well have spotted the flaw already.

The reason the windows are wet could be accounted for by other reasons. Perhaps because someone was washing the windows or a hose pipe was accidentally sprayed over them. The argument only works as a line of reasoning if we can't think of another reason for the conclusion. But the argument crumbles if we can think of another reason why the windows might be wet.

Similarly in the case of poor insulation:

It could be the case that our heating bills are high because we use a lot of power. Perhaps we have the heating on a high setting, or we seldom turn off lights, and so. It could have nothing to do with having poor insulation.

With conditional arguments what we have are some truths but a falsehood derived from them. True that if your insulation is poor your bills will be high, true your bills are high. But false you have poor insulation. So it is not enough to simply have premises in an argument that are true to have a conclusion that is true. The premises must support the conclusion.

Whenever we are confronted with an 'If …, then …' argument we need to examine them to ensure we have been offered a valid argument or merely had the initial claim affirmed. If so then we are being misled by a fallacious argument that is unsupported. The salesperson might not have knowingly misled us, but that makes it no less unacceptable.

CHAPTER 6

Another conditional argument and appeals to force

For an argument to be an argument it needs premises and a conclusion. But just because we hear a sales presentation where the argument presented has premises and a conclusion it does not follow, as we saw in the last chapter, it is a fair argument. As in the previous chapter we are often offered what merely looks like a sound argument but which is nothing of the kind. Let's deal first with another conditional argument that is fallacious.

Another conditional argument:

As in the previous chapter some arguments sound plausible when taken at face value. However, when we look at them more closely they are far from convincing. Those of us who are alert will be quick to raise an objection. Those of us not so alert will be unfairly persuaded by what amounts to empty rhetoric masquerading as an argument. Identifying spurious arguments requires we ask ourselves whether the premise or premises offered actually support the conclusion. Consider this slightly different form of conditional 'If ... then ...' argument to see whether the premise offered supports the conclusion.

> If we were paid commission on the sale, then there would be a temptation to mis-sell.
> But we do not get paid a commission
> Therefore, we don't have a temptation to mis-sell.

In this example the commission salesperson is assumed to be the only one with a motive to mis-sell. The argument once again seems plausible but this also looks like a bit of *well-poisoning*. But in addition we would be wrong to accept the conclusion on offer from the premises given. Once again the premises could be true but the conclusion false. We need only to think of other equally plausible reasons why someone might mis-sell to the public. Have they equivocated on the term 'commission' to exclude things like bonuses? Is their salary and perks performance-based?

From the consumers perspective is not a debatable point whether or not the salesperson should meet the proper requirements of sound arguments – it is incumbent upon them to do so. But even the most well-intentioned of salespeople will from time to time fail to meet these standards. We need to be vigilant in ensuring we are being offered sound arguments where the premises support the conclusion. Beware any statement that contains 'if ... then ...' *If* it does *then* you might be being led down a spurious road to a convenient conclusion.

Appeals to force:

The sort of argument which appeals to force rather than reason is not really an argument at all, rather a rhetorical ploy. So, arguments, and I use the term loosely here, appealing to force or a threat are powerful in eliciting emotions. Again, there is nothing essentially wrong with appealing to emotions unless used to persuade us at the cost of not fulfilling the proper requirements of a sound argument.

When we talk about appeals to force we are not suggesting salespeople occasional go in for a bit of arm-twisting, at least not physically. We are referring to arguments that by-pass argument and go straight to the negative consequences of inaction. For example:

> If you don't install this security system, your house will more than likely burgled.

> If you don't re-point those capping tiles you could lose the whole roof in the next storm.

> If you don't remove that tree in the front garden it will undermine your whole house.

So common is this kind of argument it hardly warrants further examples. In all such cases the utterance is an appeal to force rather than an argument based on premises and a conclusion.

Whether the use of this type of statement is acceptable practice is not the issue. The fact is they are used quite frequently in sales presentations to intimidate rather than allow us to come to a rational decision. If what the salesperson has to sell us is truly beneficial then why don't they offer sound reasons backed up by appropriate evidence? The truth has as much power to convince as a lie? If you are getting an appeal by force ask yourself why.

CHAPTER 7

Begging the question and straw man

Another source of poor argument is one that caricatures the real position making any objection raised easier to refute. Let's examine the first of two such arguments.

Begging the question:

During our discussion with a salesperson we tell them we have never taken out home contents insurance. The salesperson's response is to suggest we are obviously not concerned about our possessions. We deny the claim. The salesperson responds by stating that if we cared we would have home contents policy.

An argument commits the fallacy of *begging the question* when the truth of its conclusion is assumed by one its premises, and the truth of that premise depends for its justification on the truth of the conclusion. So, the premise asks us to grant the conclusion even before the argument is given. In other words, the salesperson is trying to smuggle into the premises of an argument the very conclusion they are trying to prove.

If we reconstruct the opening scenario it will enable us to see clearly the way in which the salesperson's line of argument *begs the question*. Initially the salesperson argued from the proposition that we don't care about our possessions together with the implicit, assumed, premise that anyone who cares would take out a home contents policy, to the conclusion if we cared we too would have home contents insurance.

But we don't have to accept the salesperson's premise that only those who have home contents insurance care about their possessions, we are not compelled to accept their conclusion that we have no concerns about our possessions. In other words, we can care about our possessions and still not have home contents insurance.

Question begging arguments come in many forms. What they have in common is they all take for granted precisely the point the salesperson should be trying to prove. But such arguments do not provide any grounds for us to accept the conclusion.

Straw man:

When we raise objections or concerns with a salesperson, like 'I want to think about it', it is common practice from them to restate the objection in another form. This practice can sometimes be helpful if the aim is to clarify our position. If for example we are unsure how a particular product might be of benefit the salesperson may restate the benefits in another way. This seems reasonable. However, it is also common practice to caricature the objection by the use of misrepresentation, exaggeration, distortion or simplification to make it easier for the salesperson to refute the objection.

By doing this they ignore our real objection to set up a weaker version. This makes the objection easier to counter thereby creating the impression the real objection has been overcome. Such tactics are known as the *straw man fallacy*.

What the salesperson is ignoring is the fact that we hold our views for genuine and sincere reasons. When we raise objections we are not simply being truculent in raising points of concern. Objections are raised because we are not convinced by the argument being presented to us. Adopting straw man tactics certainly makes the reformed objection easier for the salesperson to overcome than the real objection, but essentially it avoids the real issue. Consider the following responses to the standard objection 'I can't afford it'. 'It' of course being whatever is being offered.

> So what you are saying is that you want to live on State benefits when you retire?
>
> So you are happy to walk ten miles to the nearest service station when you breakdown?
>
> So you don't mind going through the winter with no hot water or central heating?
>
> So you are happy to keep throwing you money away on excessive heating bills?
> So you don't mind if someone slips on your drive and breaks their hip?

The response in each case is intended to suggest we are inconsistent in that we clearly want what the product does, but don't want to pay for it. Yet there need be no inconsistency on our part. It is perfectly reasonable to say we don't want to change our boiler and we want all the benefits of a boiler. Perhaps we genuinely cannot afford it, perhaps we want to get a second opinion, or perhaps we know we can get the same product cheaper elsewhere. Our objection of affordability is real and not met when the salesperson misrepresents, exaggerates, distorts, or simplifies.

The list of suggested phraseology in sales textbooks to caricature objections is endless. While this is testimony to the sales profession's inventiveness, it is also testimony to their willingness to do whatever is required to get the deal. The examples given above are quite direct and obvious, though by no means the most blatant I've witnessed. Yet any restatement of our position which caricatures rather than clarifies avoids engaging with our actual concerns. Instead it attempts to portray a more extreme or weaker position making it harder for us to defend because, in all probability, we do not advocate it.

If we are not persuaded by the proposition on offer we should not allow the salesperson to mitigate any inadequacy on their part to properly explain the proposition by adopting straw man arguments. These tactics are used for the sole purpose of making it easier for them to refute our objection and close the deal.

However, the use of straw man arguments is not confined to dealing with objections. They are often used to misrepresent any opposing view to make it easier to undermine. Suppose we are firm advocates of the National Health Service. We believe that medical treatment should be provided free at the point of delivery. The salesperson responds by asking us how we can support a system that does not treat patients on the basis of clinical need but availability. And where the treatment we are likely to receive has more to do with our postcode than the state of our health.

We might agree with the points raised, but this does not provide sufficient grounds for us to be persuaded to buy private healthcare insurance. All the salesperson has done is caricature our position and restated it in distorted or simplified form. The misrepresentation takes no account of our wider commitment to the NHS. More to the point it ignores the fact that our commitment entails more than the treatment of our own healthcare needs. It also does not deal with the fact that private health insurance will not cover emergency ambulance service, accident and emergency, routine GP visits, and so on. So while we may well agree with the deficiencies of the NHS, we can remain unconvinced that private medical insurance offers the solution.

If we are to be convinced of the virtues of a product or service the salesperson needs to provide a substantive argument, not one that misrepresents our position to make it easier for them to refute.

When we are persuaded by straw man arguments, and we often are in our daily lives, our decision will not have been based on sound argument. Rather we will have been persuaded by a misrepresentation, exaggeration, distortion or simplification of our position. This is neither acceptable practice nor necessary, especially when you consider that an honest argument also has the power to persuade.

CHAPTER 8

Red herrings and attacking the person

As consumers we are entitled to raise objections to any proposal put to us by a salesperson. However, we are often distracted from the main thrust of our argument by irrelevancies. There are also occasions when we give good reasons why we do not accept the advice being offered. Usually this is met by a counter-argument from the salesperson. However, these counter-arguments are often not as persuasive as they might at first appear. This is because they fail to distinguish between the objection and the person giving it. But let us first look at the strategy of irrelevances.

Red Herrings:

When presenting arguments it is easy to distract us from the main thrust with irrelevancies. When a salesperson comes up with an irrelevant premise as a reason for accepting their advice they commit the *red herring fallacy*. For example:

> I believe you should invest in an ISA because they are extremely popular.

Here the idea being advanced is that the ISA's popularity among the investing public is a reason why we should invest. But is this a compelling reason? If the reason we should invest is based, as it should be, strictly on the basis of its merits, combined with our needs, then its popularity is irrelevant.

Red herrings ask us to accept a particular conclusion on a questionable, irrelevant, premise. If such premises are successful it is because they seem plausible, especially when presented in a way that instils some positive attitude toward the conclusion. In this way we don't notice the irrelevancy. In the example above the inclusion of a red herring is not wrong in any ethical sense, just persuasive for the wrong reason. The example below also tries to persuade with irrelevances.

When considering the investment of a capital sum the discussion turns to the issue of security. The salesperson argues that multinationals, like their firm, offer greater security than smaller domestic companies. In this instance the premise, 'we are a multinational', is intended to make us supportive of the idea of investing with them. However, it is irrelevant. This becomes obvious if we simply asked ourselves what the salesperson would say if they worked for a smaller firm. It also ignores the fact that both small and large firms are covered by the same legislation.

Our ability to recognise red herrings depends on our knowledge of what is and is not relevant to the issue at hand. Those able to spot red herrings are not persuaded by the argument. However, for those of us who are persuaded we must not quibble over words - we have been seduced by irrelevancies.

We should keep in mind at all times that the reasons to buy should depend on a preponderance of evidence in favour of that conclusion. In the case of investing a capital sum the conclusion should be premised on our needs and the product's fitness for our purpose rather than on red herrings like the size of the company selling the product, or the products popularity, and whether or not a friend has bought a similar product, and so on.

Red herrings are simply premises that do not support the conclusion. At best they should be unpersuasive; at worst they are an attempt to intentionally distract us. In either case they should be eradicated from arguments. But sadly they probably never will be. For this reason we need to be conscious of what is, and what is not, relevant to the conclusion if we are to avoid being unfairly persuaded by red herrings.

Attacking the person:

When a salesperson addresses their response to the person, rather than an assertion or claim being made by that person, they commit the *fallacy of attacking the person.*

This type of fallacious argument is likely to surface when the salesperson is confronted with competition, or contrary advice given to us from a third party. Such tactics are questionable and do not address the issue but rather seek to justify their own claim by discrediting or attacking the person.

This fallacy appears in several forms. The first we might call abusive. Here the salesperson directly attacks you rather than the assertion you made. For example:

> You may argue that block paving is better than tarmac, but you are just following a fad.

> You may believe they offer the best deal, but you've been seduced by the adverts.

The second version of the fallacy is a circumstantial one where instead of attacking an assertion the salesperson points to the relationship between the person making the assertion and the person's circumstances. For example:

> Of course your accountant would say tax planning should only be done by them: it means more fee paying work, regardless of whether you take their advice or not.

> We really shouldn't listen to what that plumber says about the electrical wiring; their company is owned by the largest electrical contracts in the area.

The final version of the fallacy is this form of attack on the person where the salesperson turns the assertion back on the person who made it. In other words, the accusation that they do not practice what they preach. For example:

> The salesman at the Ford dealership drives a Mercedes; so I would take what he says about Fords with a pinch of salt.

The builder says you should renew your guttering; but have you seen the state of his house?

Notice that the conclusion of these arguments is left implicit, but given in the salesperson's tone. But in all of the examples the implicit conclusion has more to do with vitriol than sound reasoning.

It is also being suggested that whenever someone would benefit from something, we should reject their arguments in favour of it. This is absurd? So, it is unreasonable of the salesperson to ask us to reject a point of view just because the person or firm offering might benefit by it. What matters in each case is the strength of the reasons given irrespective of the giver gaining by it.

These types of argument should also not persuade us because they give us no more reason to accept a proposal than before we raised the initial objection.

We should be aware when an identity attack is in progress. When we experience it we need to be mindful that the character or circumstances of the person has nothing to do with the truth or falsity of the proposition being offered.

CHAPTER 9

Majority belief and perfectionists

It is not unusual for us to take our lead about what is an appropriate course of action on the basis of what the majority of reasonable people believe to be true. Many salespeople are aware of this and use this majority view as part of their argument to convince us we are taking the right course of action. After all, not everyone can be wrong, or can they? As consumers we are much more demanding than we were even a decade ago. However, when a salesperson imposes unreasonable expectations on the recommendations offered by a competitor they are not arguing fairly. But let us first look at the majority belief.

Majority belief:

Probably the most common piece of fallacious reasoning used to justify buying a product or service is to argue that because the majority of the public believe a certain proposition, then that proposition must be true. This is the *majority belief fallacy*. Taken at face value the following argument does, or at least did, seem reasonable:

> It is widely believed by most informed customers and financial experts alike that the low cost endowment is a good means of paying-off your mortgage.

However, the only reason we are given to support this recommendation is that most people believe it to be the best advice. This is not a sound argument when we examine the underlying or hidden premise of the statement above, namely:

> Any belief shared by most informed people is true.

Given the recent problems with endowment mortgages we are all wiser. But this does not mean salespeople are not prone to repeating the same mistake of making similar appeals to majority beliefs for other products.

The fallacy of majority belief is an easy one to commit, not least because quite often we can be persuaded by consensus opinion and it is quite an easy fallacy to avoid, if we want to. We should also be aware that sometimes the public have a knack of identify what is right. Being in the majority, as I said previously, doesn't necessarily make it right. But then again, it doesn't necessarily make it wrong either. Be on your guard and go with the crowd when you should, and not when you are told you should.

Perfectionist:

The perfectionist fallacy occurs when a salesperson places excessive demands on a proposal and then rejects it on the basis it will not solve the problem. This is the kind of argument we might hear used to dissuade us from taking a competitor's advice. For example:

Well I can't see how taking a few branches out of the tree will solve the problem of the roots undermining your house and weakening the foundations. Neither will it prevent the tree falling on your house if we get a storm.

I don't see how replacing a few tiles here and there and re-pointing the capping tiles will solve the structural weakness of the roof. Neither will it prevent further leaks and damage to the structure of the building.

The hidden assumption driving the *perfectionist fallacy* is that we should only pursue plans that completely satisfy our needs. In other words, no course of action is worthwhile unless it solves the problem completely. But this approach is complete nonsense. In fact if this were the basis of all recommendations we would hardly buy any products or services at all.

This is not to suggest some problems do need a complete solution. However, partial solutions form a large part of many product and service sales. Very few of us can ever afford complete solutions to problems. Many recommendations are aimed at partial rather than complete solutions and these recommendations are justified if they are part of a wider strategy to reduce the larger problem at hand.

Selling honestly does not just include being honest about what a company's products can and cannot achieve. Honesty extends to the salesperson examining their own motivation for suggesting one course of action rather than another, and this applies equally to advice given by other parties.

Understanding the absurdity of the perfectionist fallacy better enables us to defend against its use. If we hear it being used we might want to remember the following:

> Farmers put up fences around pasture to prevent the cows wandering off. Once in a while a cow escapes. But no one would fences are unjustified.

By analogy, partial solutions are justified if they resolve that portion of the problem they claim to resolve. So disparaging or rejecting a proposal simply because it is not a total solution is a weak argument.

What is required from the salesperson is a substantive argument. But even here we may still have to accept that in some instance we are better off with a partial solution rather than nothing. The salesperson dogmatically insisting that only a complete resolution is worth undertaking is not helpful.

CHAPTER 10

Weak analogies and appeals to ignorance

Using analogies in a sales presentation can aid our understanding. Yet analogies often contribute less to the argument than we might suppose. The use of an analogy might even be a ploy intended only to appeal to our willingness to acceptance the analogy, not the thing it was used to explain. Yet often analogies rely on assumptions that are wholly unreliable. There are also arguments presented to us that instead of providing a plausible set of reasons why the claim ought to be believed, the salesperson relies instead on an absence of evidence to make the case for them. While such arguments are inherently flawed they can often appear plausible when packaged in the right way.

Weak analogy:

Analogies are often used non-argumentatively in the sales process, for example, as similes or metaphors to explain something unfamiliar by comparing it to something we are likely to be more familiar with. For example, a unit trust fund may be compared to a cake: many ingredients of the cake are spread evenly throughout it. When you take a slice of cake you have some of all the ingredients not all of one. Therefore, you are never exposed to one particular ingredient. In cases such as this the analogy is not being used to establish a conclusion. However, some analogies are argumentative if they are offered to support a conclusion the salesperson wants us to accept.

There is nothing essentially dishonest with using analogies in this way, and the ability to use them reflects the richness of our language. However, the mere fact that an argument is offered in the form of an analogy often seems enough to invite immediate and irrational acceptance. This can be dishonest if the salesperson knowingly uses weak analogies.

Arguments from analogy are persuasive because they compare two situations which appear plausible similar. But while the mere utterance of an analogy tends to produce conviction many analogies do not hold up under scrutiny. As a consequence all the salesperson is doing when they use a weak analogous argument is to take an unconvincing argument and repackage it in a more persuasive form. This is dishonest for the following reason.

When a salesperson uses a weak analogy they usually argue on the basis of a proposition that if one thing is similar to another in one respect, then it is similar in a further respect. This is a mistaken inference. It does not follow that if something is similar to another thing in one respect, it is similar in all respects. A Cake is not a unit trust fund, no matter how you slice it.

There is no limit to the form analogous arguments can take; anything can be compared with anything. Life might be compared to a box of chocolates, it certainly involves a box at some point, but so far as I am aware we don't have praline centres. However, the following example is probably more useful to illustrate the point at hand:

> You wouldn't dream of not insuring your car, so why not insure your life.

This analogy claims that car insurance is like life insurance in that both offer protection. While this is true the salesperson then tries to make the claim that because both are similar, they should be treated the same in all respects.

The argument is unsound because it is obviously false to assume that a similarity in one respect implies a similarity in all respects. While it is true of course that life assurance and car insurance share some similarities, those similarities are not sufficient for the analogy to hold. In this example the dissimilarities outweigh the similarities. Life assurance has a different purpose, and you can't get arrested for not taking out a life insurance policy. Indeed, you can protect your family in any number of ways other than by buying life insurance, but you cannot protect your car without car insurance.

For an argument by analogy to be effective in giving us a reason to accept its conclusion the salesperson needs first to argue that the two things compared are sufficiently similar in the relevant respect. In other words, they must compare like with like. For example the analogy with car insurance might hold if the compared with public liability insurance.

It would of course be wrong to suppose that every analogy we hear is readily accepted. We can, and do, counter arguments based on weak analogies in a number of ways. The most likely response is for us to object that the two situations are not sufficiently similar.

Analogies might be useful for getting a point across. But for our part we must ensure that what we are being given to compare is sufficiently alike in all or at least most respects. If not we must reject the analogy. In doing so we avoid falling into the trap of accepting a weak argument repackaged in a more persuasive form.

Appeals to ignorance:

This fallacy is not strictly what its title might at first suggest. Rather it is about concluding either that because a claim has not been proven it must be *false*, or because it has not been disproven it must be *true*.

Whichever version of the fallacy is used it relies on the false assumption that either the absence of proof means it must be false, or the absence of disproof means it must be true.

Despite not offering any other reasons to support a claim, other than the fact that the claim hasn't been proved or disproved, such arguments carry persuasive force.

> There is no evidence this product is dangerous to human health.

> We have no evidence to suggest this new product will not perform better than the last.

Both arguments are as bad as each other. The first relies on the absence of a proof, and the second the absence of a disproof.

Given the fallacious nature of such arguments they have no place in a discussion intended to help us come to an informed decisions. Importantly we need to be aware that when presented with this type of argument. The mere fact that a proposition hasn't been proved or disproved is, on its own, no reason to think it false or true.

Of course the very mention of the word 'proof' suggests certainty. But there are very few things of which we can be absolutely certain. Indeed many of our decisions are not based on certainties at all. There is no certainty Tower Bridge will not collapse, but tens of thousands of commuters still cross it daily.

The important thing to remember with arguments is to make sure we are being given reasons why we should believe them, not an absence of reasons. This applies to all the varieties of arguments highlighted throughout this guide.

Steve Deery 2013

www.ingramcontent.com/pod-product-compliance
Lightning Source LLC
Chambersburg PA
CBHW070731180526
45167CB00004B/1704